Mandala Coloring Book

50 Relaxing Patterns
by 13 Artists

Mindfulness Coloring for Adults Volume 1

www.ColoringCraze.com

FREE GIFT FOR YOU!

Coloring books enthusiast? Get **Free Bonus Kit** from the site below:

=> http://www.coloringcraze.com/**bonus** <=

Test Your Colors Here

Blend Colors Here

MIX   MIX   MIX

MIX   MIX   MIX

MIX   MIX   MIX

Test Your Colors Here

Blend Colors Here

MIX ___ ___ MIX ___ ___ MIX ___

MIX ___ ___ MIX ___ ___ MIX ___

MIX ___ ___ MIX ___ ___ MIX ___

FROM THE AUTHOR

Thanks for coloring our book! I hope it was relaxing and I hope you had a lot of fun with it.

I would like to ask you for a *small* favor. Book reviews are very important for other coloring enthusiasts like you. If you have a minute, please leave a comment under our book here: **www.coloringcraze.com/review19**

It will help the buyers to make a decision and your feedback will be priceless to our illustrators ☺

All our other books are available here: www.coloringcraze.com/**our-books**

Remember to grab your **Free Bonus!**

=> http://www.coloringcraze.com/**bonus** <=

Thank You!

Made in the USA
Middletown, DE
15 May 2017